MW01366003

Other works published by the author, available from iUniverse:

An Artist's Model and Other Poems (2012)
Black Hole and Other Poems (2012)
Pursuit and Other Poems (2011)
Persistence and Other Poems (2010)
Celebrations and Other Poems (2009)
War-Wise and Other Poems (2009)
Surface Tension and Other Poems (2008)
Confusion Matrix and Other Poems (2007)

A Bell Curve and Other Poems

David J. Murray

iUniverse LLC
Bloomington

A Bell Curve and Other Poems

iUniverse books may be ordered through booksellers or by contacting:

iUniverse
1663 Liberty Drive
Bloomington, IN 47403
www.iuniverse.com
1-800-Authors (1-800-288-4677)

ISBN: 978-1-4917-0926-9 (sc)
ISBN: 978-1-4917-0928-3 (hc)
ISBN: 978-1-4917-0927-6 (e)

Printed in the United States of America.

iUniverse rev. date: 10/18/2013

Contents

Introduction

This volume is divided into seven separate sections, each devoted to a particular topic. The number of poems in each section, starting from the opening section, is 3, 9, 17, 58, 16, 12 and 3. Plotting on a graph, with sections one to seven on the horizontal axis and the number of poems in each section on the vertical axis, results in a curve rather like the familiar bell curve, but with a sharper peak than usual. The contours of the bell taper off on each side; the opening section and the final section have only three poems each.

This scheme was deliberately planned, because I am trying to present a composite snapshot of my current state of mind; in that composite, what I find myself thinking about the most is represented by the middle section (the peak of the curve), with its 58 poems. The topics of the sections will be listed in the next paragraph, but I have prefaced the whole work with a "preamble" poem titled "A Bell Curve." Each individual poem is a kind of photograph of one moment in my mental life, but putting the whole collection together under the guise of a bell curve was a conceit that allowed me to stress the unified, rather than the scattered, nature of the whole collection.

I am somewhat shy at having to confess that I have been preoccupied most recently with My Inspiration, which is the title of the longest section. The title refers not to an abstract idea but to a person, namely, the same person who served as the model in my previous book, which was titled *An Artist's Model and Other Poems* (iUniverse, 2012).

Immediately to the left side of the peak of the bell curve there is a set of 17 poems under the heading The Arts, and immediately to the right side is a set of 15 poems under the title Other Musings—which is about other women in my life who have not left my thoughts and about whom I felt motivated to write what you read here.

Then, further down the left side of the bell curve, there are nine poems under the heading Psychology and Philosophy, which reflect my professional interests in these. Further down the right side of the bell curve are 12 poems about the vistas I see from the balcony of the apartment I moved into about four years ago, which is located on a clifftop near Toronto. This section is titled Space and Sky.

Finally, bringing up the tails, so to speak, of the bell curve are, on the left, three poems under the heading Children, and on the right, three poems under Memorials that are additional to those contained in *Celebrations and Other Poems* (iUniverse, 2009). These concern my deceased wife, *née* Esther Mongrain (1944–2009). Her ashes are buried in the Cataraqui Cemetery, in Kingston, Ontario. This cemetery is a scenically attractive resting place that happens to lie only a short distance from the Kingston train station, as is hinted in the middle poem of the section. Kingston itself is located about halfway between where I now live, Toronto, and where she used to live, Montréal.

The section on children opens with a happy memory of a day at the zoo with my grandchildren and their parents, and the section ends with an equally happy memory of my own grandfather, possibly the kindest person I ever met. The middle poem, titled "Ancient and Modern," is based on an actual event I witnessed in a wonderful park, the Guild Inn Park, which is located a stone's throw from where I live. In the next section, on psychology and philosophy, each poem speaks for itself.

In the section titled The Arts, several poems require some explanation. In the first poem, "Thinking of London," the line "talking of Klimt, not Michelangelo" is a take-off of T. S. Eliot's lines:

> In the room the women come and go
> Talking of Michelangelo.

These lines appear twice in his poem "The Love Song of J. Alfred Prufrock" (1917). Eliot wrote them almost a century ago, and it is true that the vividly coloured and fantastically ornate paintings of Gustav Klimt (1862–1918) have received massive attention only recently, although nearly all of them had been painted before Eliot wrote about Prufrock. I was amazed to find that Klimt did not even get an entry in several works of general reference from the 1970s.

A series of eight poems consists of homages to writers of the past. J. A. Strindberg (1849-1912) was a Swedish poet and playwright who wrote about every aspect of angst imaginable in family and marital situations, as well as in his own experiences of delusional disorder. The word *kvinnar* in the text is Swedish for "women."

In his later years, A. E. Housman (1859–1936) was the Professor of Latin at Trinity College, Cambridge, but his book of poems titled *A Shropshire Lad* (1896) was already being widely read by the generation younger than his, and his verse continues to appeal to young people nowadays. Many of his poems consist of a few four-line stanzas, with a lilt and a musical quality unique to Housman.

Thomas Mann (1875–1955) was a German novelist who not only won the Nobel Prize in Literature for 1929, but also voluntarily left Germany for Switzerland in the early 1930s when he realized the potential extent of the Nazi threat. He was particularly intrigued by the "loner" psychology of the dedicated artist. The "modern book" referred to in the second stanza of the poem is *Art and Madness: A Memoir of Lust without Reason*, by Anne Roiphe (New York: Doubleday, 2011).

Charles P. Baudelaire (1821–67) wrote stunning sonnets in French about romance in general and his own romances in particular. The title of his book *Les Fleurs du Mal* (1857) can be translated as "Flowers of Evil." My poem is dedicated to the memory of Mrs. Patricia Soberman, who once made a study of Baudelaire's work, and whose patronage, as well as that of her lawyer husband, Daniel Soberman, was greatly appreciated in Kingston literary and musical circles.

Stephen J. Leacock (1869–1944) was the chairman, from 1908 to 1936, of the Department of Economics and Political Science at McGill University in Montréal. But he is much better remembered as a humorist. I discovered his 1911 book titled *Nonsense Novels* when I was a teenager browsing hungrily through the holdings of the Cheadle Public Library (near Manchester in the United Kingdom). In a 1913 essay titled "Homer and Humbug: An Academic Suggestion," Leacock pointed out that if *he* had written the following lines back in Greek or Roman times, he would have been world-famous:

> Thus does the race of man decay or rot
> Some men can hold their jobs and some cannot.

Heinrich Heine (1797–1856) wrote in German, but he lived most of his life in Paris, where he specialized both in a rhythmic kind of blank verse and in short, rhyming love poems, often only a handful of stanzas long. Much of my poetry reflects his influence, which I absorbed by a kind of undeliberate osmosis when I first discovered his work. He has been acknowledged as having provided lyrics for many a *Lied* (a German art-song) and being a precursor, in his mastery of brief, laconic verse forms, of A. E. Housman.

J. W. von Goethe (1749–1832) lived to be 83, and during his lifetime he contributed not only to small-scale poetry but also to large-scale drama (e.g., *Faust*) and to the development of the German novel. But what attracts me to Goethe in particular is his interest in science. He can validly be said to have contributed, though not always accurately, to the theory of how we see colours and to the question of whether the skull might have evolved as a specialized form of vertebra. It is this side of Goethe that I have highlighted in my homage to him.

The poetry of Alfred Lord Tennyson (1809–1892) was so famous in his lifetime that he was knighted by Queen Victoria and made the successor to William Wordsworth in the role of her poet laureate. His work was unjustly underestimated in the early twentieth century, because it was idealistic rather than impressionistic, and romantic rather than down-to-earth. But his writings, along with the paintings of the pre-Raphaelite movement, epitomized the near-idolatrous worship, typical of Victorian male artists, of attractive women; these men strove to know where they stood in the great cauldron of society, and they were honest about their anxieties in a way I have never failed to admire. Tennyson finished one of his poems with the lines

> The moan of doves in immemorial elms
> And murmuring of innumerable bees.

This deserves a standing ovation from the angels. The quotation is from Tennyson's very long collection of connected poems titled *The Princess* (5th edition, 1853).

Comments need only be given to two poems in the long central sequence titled My Inspiration. The poem titled "Byronic" directly quotes the line "She walks in beauty, like the night" that opens a short lyric poem by Lord Byron (1788–1824). At the end of the poem titled "Against the Grain," I wrote that I

> could not think of a single way
> Both Right and Good.

The last line is a reference to a classic treatise on ethics by W. D. Ross titled *The Right and the Good* (Oxford at the Clarendon Press, 1930). No annotations are needed for the two final sections, Space and Sky, and Memorials.

As well, I want to thank Marissa E. Barnes, MA, and Rachel Murray, MLIS, for their help in preparing this work for publication with iUniverse.

Preamble: A Bell Curve

Each photograph I take, in words,
Of what I'm thinking here and now,
Gets juggled into its opposite when
I shoot that mental snap again;

And, often, a moment's caricature
Of absent-minded concentration
Can melt to a blob of sheer pretence
At normalness and common sense;

And, likewise, a pause for a hope or a dream
Can be pulled to a near-insanity
When that hope or dream is starkly struck
By a flame-shot fired by Lady Luck;

And so, in these poems, I've tried to fix
My slippery thought-streams into a mix
Of time-fused photographs of my mind,
A bell curve of heartbeats intertwined.

Children

At the Zoo

I sigh and count the minutes' soulful hours;
Time, like today, can pass and sunny be.
Contentment lies in a child's contented hands
Who walks with a Popsicle with her parents and me,
While the sun shines down on territorial lands
Where treasures bask in baskets bathed in flowers.

Contentment lies in the slow-unfurling necks
Of giraffes who idly chew as they watch the crowd,
Or the slow inforwarding of a camel's knees
As it strolls its walk with its youthful rider proud
Of his haughty height and his power to highly please
His upstaring parents, although he's only six.

And so, in contentment, can days pass by
While I count their minutes' soulful hours and sigh.

Ancient and Modern

Back in the raucous years of empty youth,
I plagued the globe with curiosity;
I went to where the ancients pried the truth
From what they thought oracular, the sky,
And the pitiable wastes of falling day.

So Rome I saw, whose untopped columns stood
For money and for roads that combed the fields;
And Greece I saw, whose temples, once of wood
But now of stone, were carved to timber shapes
Intended as more enduring monuments;

And of Ephesus a portalled library
That stood as symbolic epitaph of Life,
Masquerading as idolatry,
Welding the Greek Diana's archery
To a new religion, Christianity;

And everywhere, on fallen sculpted stones
That spread their placid flatness to the sun,
Adorned with roundels and medallions,
Heaped into cascades of broken artefacts
Of cavalcaded masonry and rocks,

Everywhere I saw, spread out on ledges,
Living lizards with lidded eyes and lanky
Tails, soaking up sun, as they had done
From ages when the town had suffered sieges
Till now, when tourists, packed on adult cruises,

From irreligious universities came,
From campus towns across the dappled West,
To see the sources of ancient fallacies
And superstitions crowned with uncouth Beauty,
And words that smoothed a soothing way to Science.

Later, in Canada, when the banks had grown
And folded the modern world into their armoury,
Their buildings had their pedestal stone fronts embellished
With sculptures of porticos Grecian and graciously furnished
With keystones and columns and carvings that clearly established

A heritage of antiquity magnified;
And, later still, when those buildings were uprooted,
Doomed to be rubble 'midst towers of steel and glass,
Some of their treasured carvings were removed,
On the backs of trucks that just withstood their weight,

To a park on Toronto's edge, where one now sees,
Through vibrant pines and firs and sky-lit trees,
Porticos like the porticos of Rome,
Columns like the portals of Greek libraries,
And grey-cut half-height columns in the grass;

And I saw two girls, near-teenagers, climb up
Onto a grey-cut half-height quasi-plinth,
Modelling, with their limber *mouvements*,
Ur-ancient rites of life-a-giving lore,
Unscripted, upon those stones from yesteryear.

What My Grandfather Said

When I was young and aged about twelve,
By Edinburgh's shore,
My grandfather went out one night
And didn't return before

The midnight hour, it was, I think;
Kindly as ever he was;
I had been finishing reading a book,
And was pleased he'd come back because

I didn't have to wait up for him now;
I could flop my weary head
On the drowse-inducing pillows and sheets
Of my comfortable bed;

But suddenly he stopped to talk,
Bending his face down to mine;
I could see the bald crescent of his head
With its opalescent shine;

And he said to me quite quietly,
As if a confidence
He wanted to impart to me
But felt some diffidence:

"Be careful of strong liquor, lad;
Avoid it when you can;
You must only rarely drink when you
Grow up to be a man."

As he said this all the while his face
Was poised so close to mine
That the smell on his breath was obvious,
But it can't have been of wine,

For only beer and Scotch I'd seen
When visitors came to call;
And this was the first time in my life
I'd known him to smell at all.

And so I remembered what he'd said.
The words above aren't correct;
Their gist is there, but his breath smelled so good
It seduced my intellect.

Psychology and Philosophy

Human Outliers

Bleak and out of kilter with their time,
Outliers are tempted into crime
Or maybe feel a force to write in rhyme.

Oh, for a normal's platitudinous calms!
Oh, for a saint's propensities to psalms
That offer soporific cooling balms

All in a heinous eagerness to please
Divinities whose edicts feed the trees
And cap the skies with high infinities!

So, idly I fashion and calibrate these lines:
Either divinity encompassed bad designs;
Or humans strove to stem their own declines;

Or laws of genetics functioned hit-or-miss,
Engendering human runts who vent like this.

Nature's Sway

How, in a world so rayed with gorgeous colours,
Can any thought of darkness dim the day?
A lucent, faintly yellow, sort of blue
Covers the sky, but a cloud flat seems to say
That its darkness will not go; it's here to stay.

Although some incompetent ruler of the world
Might argue that he or she knows every way
To trim the indulgent, or to puff the small,
The fact remains that Nature wields its sway
To ensure that, however gorgeous its display,

Life will go on, with reasonable chances
That manoeuvring outweighs what dark advances
Threaten to tilt composure into anger
Without which darkness never poses danger.

A Shopworn Day

When is a broad, bright new display
Symbolic of a brighter day?

When the broadness of the light
Signifies an end to night;
When the brightness of the red
And yellow leaves unfolds to spread
Its active colours on as yet
Untreated treetops, dull and wet;

But the trees still lie open in the park,
Not only to the mist and dark,
But also to a sun grown cold
And bored and tired and worn and old,
Symbolic of a shopworn day
That failed to chase the clouds away.

I Have No Time

I have no time for simple games or pastimes;
If it's not serious, life-or-death, or work,
I feel I waste my time and lose the spark
That energizes all I undertake;

And so, I lose some women with my ardour;
I'm so eager-keen to over-tout my wares
That warranted suspiciousness upflares
And people avoid approaching me with offers;

And so aware am I of my social drawbacks
That sometimes I dress too over-formally,
Trying to make people think I'm that way normally,
When all I'm trying to do is act acceptably;

And, worst of all, although I always try
For musicality in poetry,
I've grown so to dislike all noisy revelry,
That a Saturday night with nothing to do is heavenly.

Early Morning Train #1

A rising sun can look as if it sinks
When, on the train, I'm heading to a place
Where, on the one hand, ecstasy might wait,
On the other, I might lapse into disgrace;

And so, bewildered by uncertainties,
I settle down to the paper and look away
From the window, to what it is I'm trying to read,
Hoping my hopes will rise, not sink, today.

Lingering

To linger long in empty pleasure
Is not to re-court loneliness;
Each preparation shows endeavour
To perpetrate ambitiousness
Into hours of lingering leisure.

Nature is king, but also queen
Of the domain of her high command;
There, beneath Venus' gown, unseen,
Lie spreads of open wonderland;
And none of your lingering will have been

A wasteful chore in a chariot-bed,
Pulled by capricious horses across
A waste-lot sky demerited;
Your lingering longing never will be lost,
But win you storm-felt happiness instead.

Parties

No matter how grimly a fellow first reveals
That he is not immune to those appeals
That are offered by women who participate
In social occasions, he will accumulate
More social worth if he brings a female guest,
To help him move and mingle with the rest
Of the couples who roam the room and laugh
At beams of banter and amusing chaff;
Happy to show that they are couples firm—
But meanwhile succeed in making that fellow squirm
And fall to a child-like voice in deference
To their mutual ease and mutual reverence—
Shame will apportion him when witless he stares
At someone's wife, while his female guest just glares.

Lightning Storm

Almighty forces, busting their belt-buckle sky,
Proclaim, in ravenous verses, that there's no reason why
Reason should not remove its raiments to score
A shimmer of glamorous madness for evermore.

For only when reason has done its best to kill
Whatever amorous feelings grow in us still,
Does lightning flash its belabouring, arrogant sword
To delete from our nightmares every belligerent word.

After a Miserable Winter

Mostly, the greens are from the conifers
That stood stout-heartedly through the winter's cold;
Lawns are dull brown from soaking snow and seepage,
And flowers are far too small to see from here:
A vantage point for macro-worlds magnificent;
And yet a whisper in this soft-sighed air,
Something not of cold, but of incipience,
Suggests that buds are starting to embrace
The many-coloured branches of the spring,
And that new life, iconic in its reference
To life, albeit new or dark or coloured,
Has started to salve all conscience from the air,
And thereby to communitize the cells
That, animal-like, are jettisoning death.

The Arts

Thinking of London

Sometimes a nightfall takes so long to fall
That darkness's dangers seem imperceptible;
Time lasts so long it's indestructible,
And Death seems to play no part in this at all.

I can look out feeling—well, unfree,
(Because no booze or bubbly am I allowed)
When I lunch in teashops that rarely see a crowd,
At tables where elderly ladies sip their tea,

Talking of Klimt, not Michelangelo,
Watching their elderly selves slip slowly off
To a delicate land where, still, Rachmaninoff
Gives them a voice that tells them where to go

When humdrum falls like Lucifer from the sky,
And noisiness rakes its gravel over the streets,
And rickety textings, camouflaged by tweets,
Send trivia where Tennyson once rode by.

The Social World

No brutal, worrying grindstone do I bear
On which to whet an axe of sheer despair
That sometimes cuts into my *joie de vivre*
With nothing but sad tidings to deliver,

Namely, the place of inequality
In a social world that's veined with cruelty,
Because what most men want is easy to name,
But what most women want is not the same.

One answer to this drastic difference
Is for men to modify their pure impatience,
By raising sentiments to gilded arts
And hiding angers deep within their hearts;

And timing their minds so that the world's imbued,
For kindness's sake, with wantonness subdued.

Homage to Strindberg

A poet is a miscreant made
From sinner and from saint.
He brandishes a fervent spade
On myth without complaint;
But let the Truth peer in the door,
And he's corrupt and taint.

A poet is a lackey made
From a saint and from a sinner.
Goodness spreads its masquerade
Within him like a winner;
But respect's so cold it maddens him
And makes him fear all *kvinnar.*

No poet was e'er an offspring true
Of his father and his mother.
Whatever they'd wanted him to do
Would inspiration smother;
And wherever he finished in the end,
His goal had been some other.

And no poet ever quite fulfilled
The dreams of his mother and his father;
Ruefully his words he'd spilled
On anyone who'd bother
To befriend him and to hold him tight,
To keep his souls together.

Homage to Housman

The Attic verse of golden Greece
Can seize a handful of the brain
And turn it upside down to show
It won't be right way up again;

And the rhymes of stodgy-hearted Rome
Have little more than fumes and grace
To strain and filter out desires
Into a dry, but dignified, place;

But when I think of thee, my lad,
My thoughts go thundering, far away
From Greece and Rome, to the placid peace
Of an English farm on an English day.

Homage to Thomas Mann

The peak of madness is reached when all one's work
Becomes too single-minded to be borne;
Prizes and rewards go to the jerk
Who wants to drink and sleep his way around;
No wonder the inborn artist feels forlorn,
When he or she can find no common ground.

I've just read a book on madness and on art
By a writer who'd fill the vacant slot
Of "muse" to a playwright; but her generous heart
Could not be happy in a world of drinkers,
Who stressed and claimed it was their rightful lot
Through "freedom," to "find themselves" as "artist-thinkers";

Thereby, they claimed, they'd find themselves for real
And harbour cocooning novels, poems, or plays,
Or sculpted works, or paintings that appeal
To the rich, who'd feed the "artists" with real food,
And fatten their bank accounts and stuff with praise—
Reviews on which they'd base their livelihood;

And, through these appalling junctions of pure stress,
Our authoress, as yet unfamed, kept on,
Aiming to give to others such redress
As she could give, with hand or hope or purse,
And try to reverse their blunt oblivion,
And shield them from rejection or from worse.

Her playwright she married, but "inspired" (he said),
He would saunter, clutching *her* cash, quietly out
Into the night (while she remained in bed),

Claiming (he said) to be "inspired" by bar
Or brothel, while she, resistant to all doubt,
Assumed that his growing art would take them far.

A baby came; "her child" it's called throughout
Her book on art and madness, where "her child"
Is everywhere; "her child" cries out and screams
If she leaves the room to join the other guests,
At a party at George's where she's reconciled
To no longer being astonished at requests

To make the evening eloquent with gin,
Or let a stranger place his sweaty hand
On her thigh, as if she'd later let him in
To her oh-so-mature, sophisticated stance,
Where love is not possessive; nothing is banned
From the mutual duetting in this dance;

And her playwright husband, there across the room,
Talks in enticing ways of Gide or Proust
To somebody's wife who's trying to hide the gloom
Of her mental homeliness from would-be flirts
With would-be giftedness, who tried to boost
Their would-be minds by fingering her skirts.

So she left all that for her child's sake and renewed
Her staider earlier ways; for Thomas Mann,
Society could be worse than solitude;
And art that was worlds away from what she'd known
Could foster and distil a future plan,
Where nobody feared to reap what they had sown.

Homage to Baudelaire (In Memoriam Patricia Soberman)

No curse of mine is strong enough to stain
A strengthened wall of Light bereft of pain,
For Light is what upholds the fortress wall
That shelters all the arts for one and all;

Yet Darkness also holds a velvet plate,
On which lie artefacts of greed and hate,
And sometimes the Darkness holds a chandelier
That throws a light on what is not quite clear:

Namely, the "evil" in *Les Fleurs du Mal*,
Which never is *really* lacking in morale,
But, rather, rouses thoughts inapposite
Made soft by sonnets cast from sound and light.

These span the passing years and, even now,
Bewitch us without our understanding how.

Homage to Stephen Leacock

Oh, to be normal, now that winter's here!
I never go skiing; all I do is fall.
When I walk in the snow, I get too tired too soon,
And shopping's exhausting; I always get too hot.

I only feel normal, when the winter's near,
At a table, with pen and paper, filling all
The space I want with lines that I write down,
Knowing that some will work, and some will not.

Homage to Heinrich Heine

The night that swept the storm and grey away
Opens the dawn that starts another day,
And there, on the railings, hangs a bold array
Of glistening raindrops that seem to want to stay.

Still life is an art form never far from death;
A glistening raindrop seems to hold its breath,
While asking, "Why do I live and do not drown?"
Before the laws of physics pull it down.

Homage to Goethe

Out from my endless storminess of mind
Drop some equations. Oh, please don't condescend
To say they are "nice" or "clever" or "refined";
They might be poisonous for humankind.

Ethics must trump all scientific dust;
A truth that's true might still be too unjust
To promulgate in little magazines
Or spread in student cafes and canteens

By poets, who seek equations to explain
Why nobody reads their poems, or complain
That the Truth they had hoped to find in synthesis
Of Science, clasped in high romantic bliss,

Had ended in a blind uncertainty
That rubbed its shoulders with insanity.

Homage to Tennyson

I am almost mad with the beauty of women;
There is no name for this constricting band
That ties my hands to my stiff yet tremulous sides,
Yet out-releases furies that command
All tender enterprises to be cool and bland,
Tactful and moderate—while Beauty herself derides
Such subtle and empty cowardice and brands
Me as overweak, and with a woman's hands.

The beauty of women batters me to sane;
Nothing's of deeper depth than is the kill
To a hunter's mind, crawling its way to its goal,
The never-lasting consummating thrill
Of an arrow set to propel itself, until
It falls, with a bloodstain, into the very soul
Of the prey. But a poet hunts with only one thought:
How to envelop Beauty without getting caught.

Early Morning Train #2

When, on the train, the rhyming lines
Hum into tune with the engine's wheels
And captured are by a moment's pen,
The writer inwardly stammers and reels.

Yet all of the while, as he looks out the window,
Not seeing the fields or the grasses for yearning,
The rhythm is strengthening, giving him force
To stop the old darkness from ever returning.

To Music

I want to retire and lick my unpurified wounds,
And the only religion that seems to give a damn
Has Beethoven, *qua* doctor, doing the daily rounds.

Mist Tops

I see the mist tops forming on the hill,
But fail to see what forms they symbolize;
Either they're hiding what they compromise
And want to keep secret from my prying eyes,
Or they are warning, like solemn deep-sea voices,
That curiosity's the worst of poets' vices;

And so I watch the sun descend beyond
The grey that cloaks the hilltop's upper shoulder;
The grey dictates that, though I'm growing older,
I should take care, lest temptation make me bolder.
The grey makes sure I do not know what waits
Beyond Desire's barriers and gates.

Uplifted

I heard a wondrous operetta song
In which I'll swear one note was truly wrong,
But it worked to lift that ditty to sublime
And consecrated to the end of time.

I've heard that done before in a serious *Lied*
Wherein the millstream's waves converged to greet
A dying poet's waving hair as he drowned;
That note uplifted "pretty" to "profound";

And trivial though it be to those with thought,
The aggregate of single moments caught
In my music memory's ideology
Seems near-momentous to *my* thinking me,

Because two shafts of ever-burning light
Can aggregate to beacons burning bright
Illuminating Dark-time's conflagration
And dazzling it to dead with subjugation.

Moping

I never thought I'd write a work that grew,
Unfused by any long anticipation
That what I wrote endeared itself to you,
Or you, or you, who played participation
In my erotic, or sclerotic, dreams;

But this is a work wherein my scientist-self,
Reaching for stars where Galileo sleeps,
Reformulates that law unto himself;
The stars are tears the cosmos slowly weeps
When faced with unavoidable extremes

According to which most poets cannot tell
Why love should be, for poets, such a hell,
And yet continue with experiments
In which their footprints grow to continents.

Future Imperfect

As though upon the surface of the Earth there moved
A secret power to minister new cures imperative,
So there moved into his words an overt felony,
A rigorous crime, a scheme of plots conjectured,
A rhythm of exasperated foe,
And rhyme of insidious hatchings of revenge.

So it is that all perfections fade;
No character, no buildup of the good and ethical,
No fleeced perfection heals a wolf in lambskin.
Even the hoary platitudes of age,
Which turn the tides of fury with their ice,
Cannot suffice to fix and still perfection.

But Nature can outperform all platitudes;
And Art can outwit all beatitudes.

Times

Days
Perpetrate the bombshell dawns
That evening
Spawns.

Months
Destroy the venal arts
That night
Imparts.

Years
Wipe out the memories
Of awful
Centuries.

My Inspiration

An Artist's Model Goes to Press

Today has full achievement finished
A task begirt with stars;
No stress has stolen any strength,
And you're now free to parse
And deconstruct whatever words
Are trash from gender wars;

Peace I have found with its attainment;
I look at it and view
You springing, surgent, from its lines,
Almost an ingénue,
Resplendent with assertiveness
That really suits your *you*;

And any real-life flaws in my ideal
Only make it more fervent and more real.

The Forest and the Trees

Although I see the forest *and* the trees—
They wave and bend in the blows of the breathy breeze—
Each tree is a stalwart blockage of my aim
Of an arrow I want to penetrate her heart
To prove to her I need her for my art;

And if these lines seem overblown and trite,
They nonetheless feel just exactly right
To me, for whom romance is not a game,
But not a contest either, waged o'er nothing;
It's something warmly comforting and soothing;

And only a forest can feel the total whole
Of the flight of arrows flooding from my soul.

Accident

I see these drenching colours on the wall
Of the hill, a synthesis of subtle fall,
And feel my heartbeat stop and stutter and stall.

Because their beauty is an accident,
Coincidence of a sunlight's incident
Angle upon the sloping hill's ascent,

Exorbitant would be a proclamation
That all of this was for your delectation,
When two more minutes brings acceleration

Of the fading of those colours into fawn:
The colour of dead leaves in early dawn,
Before the sun has risen and has drawn

His golden chariot across the sky
To energize the colours standing by.

Town and Gown

In universities there are more men
Of modest height and brain-entrained, like me,
Than there are tall and magisterial;
But cities, where offices and finance reign,
Are far more full of stereotypes like these:
Strong and encouraging trust, with deepened voices;
While occasional women, tribal deep at heart,
Confess to greater interest in a dullard
Than in some scholar trying to impress.

But you, my golden girl, with honey'd tongue
And loosened hair that falls to kiss your arms,
Are paragon of the comprehensible;
You spread your radiant thought-streams on the air,
Leaving your host-admirer, me, astounded.

Now Winter Comes

Now winter comes, intrepidly, on foot,
Ready to plunder summer's passing glow;
The northern wind is strong and starts to blow
Its icy signs of provenance about.

The sky is colder-looking than last week,
The clouds seem clearer in a crystal light;
Each morning steals more darkness from the night;
Each evening steals in earlier than I seek;

And why should I not profit from September?
Its falling leaves kaleidoscope its days;
A growing threat of snow begins to faze
Those who have gleaned a summer to remember;

And colours resynthesized from autumn's heart
Are flaunted by your clothing's sumptuous art.

Unyielding

A day, so filled with fog it seemed to fade,
Eventually reached an evening's misty nastiness,
Which suddenly came bright with flashing lightning,
While booms that roared like sonic thunderscapes
Careened and crashed their way across the clouds;

And that great brightness, with its welcome roars,
Lured me awake to contemplate the fog
That falls upon my days when you're away
And fills each corner of each thinking hour
With hidden clouds that overshade pure thought;

But my "pure thought" is not the kind of "pure"
That others think of; it is more primeval
In the way it pushes, into art and English,
Panoplies of pure passion, where the "pure"
Refers to its unyielding monotone.

Depth

Deep in the darkest depths of night
My thoughts sneak down to play
With the physical state of all my mind
That tells me you won't go away;

For I love you deeper than Danäe,
Stronger than Phoebus's sun,
And longer, I think, than Attica's shore,
Whose cliffs and coves go on and on.

Counterfactual Conditional

A bright-lit mist that furs the lake's far edge,
Blending admixtures of water and the sky,
Seems far too ready to weasel itself inside
A poem to make it redolent of why
The only sound it sings is a silent cry;

And a mist that clouds that distant anchorage
Would be welcomed, if I knew I still could try
To view that mist as benevolent biocide
That blurred the pains from times I thought I'd die
And left to Time new anaesthesiae.

Fearful Odds

A splotchy sky, so terrible in splendour
That wonder-making people think of gods,
Can nevertheless make people with more gender
Refuse to countenance such awful odds;

And yet, like all that Nature spreads around us,
It moves and prods my mind to think of you;
Live miracles like you can quite confound us
When they drive away our minor thoughts like dew;

And so we pursue an overcold reality;
Imagination's ploys are stilled and stalled;
We fight to ensure that nothing like banality
Will ever crush what dreams our minds enthralled;

For little is worse than to sense that a dream,
Quiescent, might be running out of steam.

As I Read the Morning Paper

I see, in a simple world
As I read the morning paper,
A glimpse of your imaged face,
And stop the reading I must.

I dash to the table, where awaits
My pen to scamper down these words,
Because you've blasted, with your beauty,
All of my lassitude on this,

A sunny morning, where I and my morning paper
Were wasting, well, years of sunny seconds,
And what I wrote was a simple admission of verity;
I hoped that the distillation of my time

Would scatter its Alexandrines over every seascape,
Landscape, airscape, I might have to view without you.

I Do Not Want

I do not want to speak anxieties
That I, by others, too easy am to take
Advantage of, and off me gloatings make,
While I, for romance's sentimental sake,
Dare contemplate neither final rest nor break.

I dare not dream that somehow common sense
Will lift its wretched arm to snap your spell,
So nourishing and real I cannot tell
What's dream and what is not, or to dispel
What fantasies had raised my hopes until

A mighty wall, unbreached, stood thick and fast
Whose *raison-d-être* was to block the past,
Unless a pain appeared that breached that wall
And rendered me helpless to Memory's arsenal.

A Setting Sun

I cannot supersede a setting sun
I can't outrun;
I tread a placid water, where I stand
Away from land;
I look at the mighty sunset-laden sky
And wonder why
I made my awful blunderbuss-mistake;

You *did* forsake
My company, except when science called
And enthralled;
Except when work could be remunerated
And tolerated;
Except when you were tempted to read my books
And I your looks;
Except all times in which a setting sun
Spelled union.

Sunshine and Warmth

Though showers bereave the silent countryside
Here and there, with cloud-gaps in between
Of speckled sunshine and of patchy warmth,
The sun will always shine, with permanence,
Wherever you spread essentiality
About this bitter little bit of Earth
Whereon I mend the patchwork of my days.

And though those clouds and skies refill that earth
Each day with their brooding colours of the north,
They will always seem mirrored, angled down
To where I look at them, with silent eyes,
In their high caparison'd, gloried cumuli
Or dressed with ephemeral feather-sided wings;
They shout to me that you outnumber them.

Death Wish?

No higher form of death can come to us
Than a scrappy farewell on a gusty evening
Where clouds are the messengers of downpours
And infinite moonscapes backgrounds for defeat.

No moderate form of death can stoop to sweep
All decadence from my lonely lust for you,
Because such moderation *is* a death
That desecrates all higher calls to union.

No lower form of death can come to us
Than a veil of paterfamilias counterparts,
Of greetings and hypocrisies of laymen
Poised at the pews wherein they never worship.

The only form of death I want for me
Is one where I write for you, eternally.

Anxieties

I make new partings multiply,
Like locusts in a field;
A brazen emptiness hints that I
My gifts have failed to yield;
And the apertures of a summer sky
Have doorways blocked and sealed.

The sun shines everywhere but here,
With a heat I could enjoy;
The skies are exceptionally clear
When they my hopes destroy;
And a signalling cloudbank fails to steer
Me from the ancient ploy

Of flirting with some laggard lass
Who'd help me to surpass
The grief I'd feel at loss of you,
If she were to undo
The knot that had pulled my heartstrings tight
The day that you took flight.

Jaded

Impossible embellishments
Score the written signs
That indicate developments
Embedded in these lines;

And rotary wheels of black-lit nights
Scatter themselves across
The formulaic sounds and sights
Of lyrics that mourn a loss;

And different melodious antonyms
Regress to meaninglessness
Whenever a poem's rueful rhymes
Incarcerate carelessness.

Oh, what a pain a verse like this
Can be to one who dares
To calculate what was "hit" or "miss"
In blunderbuss'd affairs.

What I Feel

I know of nothing that need paralyze
My looking lightly at your eyes
As they flash, from their open spheres,
Indubitable tears.

Nor need I desist from saying that your voice
Would even make a handsome prince rejoice
To think he knows your mind,
Because your voice sounds kind;

But I can only stammer what I feel
When, given your overpowering appeal,
I crave a chance to start,
Again, to move your heart.

Past Imperfect

I am o'erclamoured with the power of emptiness;
Poised and waiting for you to take your leave, I saw
A chair in the hallway and, contrary to my custom,
Was pushed by a downward draught of sudden depressiveness
To sit down slowly on it; all the time you watched,
Wondering perhaps what stress had taken its hold,
What flurry of flat effort had given such a push
For me to sit instead of standing to see you off.
I was abased by an anger vented on myself;
A mistake had been made when, at the very final minute,
I had switched from tactic A to tactic B, mistakenly
Thinking B would be more impressive to your eyes;
But you were upset because you were thereby overloaded.

I am so tired of being imperfect, when perfection
Permeates your looks and general mien, while imperfections
Cloud the weather and your conditions of work; I feel
I move from being me to being a *Ding an sich*
Among the ranks of things you do not crave.

La Belle Dame Avec Merci

No higher mercies crown the firmament
Than that which made you merciful at birth;
You were true Verity's accomplishment
When first you visited this graceless Earth,
Armed with the senses of a deity;

And "eloquence" is far too poor a word
To properly hymn how much I praise your worth;
So I'll proclaim your generous accord
To flocks of birds that volley back and forth,
With admirable impropriety,

Beating their wings on silent walls of wind,
And cawing impeccable hunt songs to the air
As they careen on wind-drifts that rescind
All gravitational laws; those birds declare
They'd have no patience with my blunt sobriety.

This Sporting Life

Are there no sports to stay my honest longing
To hold you in arms of ice, instead of hot,
Because I view you, kindly, as belonging
To a wide world that welcomes the wanton not?

There *is* a sport that pulls me into it:
Poetry's wisdom is hale, and kind enough is
To weld, using solders of armoured gold and wit,
Matter and Mind to a throne of ineffable images.

Soliloquy

How dare cold Death upbraid me for being kind?
In amicality between the genders
I have upheld a sacrosanct belief;
But only a short extension of my empathy
To those, as I was, bereft of the readily physical
Has left a noisy burden of disdain,
A quasi-annoyance with unseemly blandness,
That stirs the confection of my gangren'd soul
Into a deeper sympathy for men
And women who, like me, seek out to find
Friendly amusements with equally amorous minds,
And knowledge forethought of those minds' achievements;
But slowly each feels a falling of the crest
At the common-sense sobriety of the social,
And the withering wonderings of other minds
At the single-mindedness of those like me
Who see, in lively flesh accompanied
By curious and intemperate kinds of wit,
Virtuousness and Truth personified.

Fingering the Wind

I wait for the silent verdict of your team
Of warrior-defencemen judging me
And yet am surreptitiously inclined
To be at ease with the present status quo
Of genial stance of superficial standoff.

I wait for the fall's new brilliant colours' shine.
The burstings into scarlets of that tree
That, a month ago, was first to groom its glow
From faded russet to spectacular red
Seem like renewals of my summer longings.

If the seasons change, then maybe, so can you.
Fingering the wind to see which way
It blows, I wait for one autumn hue to deface
At least one breastplate of one warrior
Defending your intractability.

When the Winds Begin

When the winds begin, the waves to speckle start;
A sort of movement massive, but impassive,
Shifts across the outspread surface, grey,
Just like a cloud, but not; a current blown
By the winds' beginnings, ploughing up a bold
New riverlet of whitecaps across the top
Of the greying lake, the darkening sea of water,
To where the lakeshore's boulders start and stop.

This speeded movement signals that I speed up
My bold and speeded movement in on you;
Too long I have waited, patient but impatient,
For you to smile enhancement harmlessly
Down on me where, guilelessly, I sat
While you stood up, a move to move past me.

Tarnished

I cannot tarnish what I do not know;
In vain I'd try to count affinities
Between the thought-erected continents
That symbolize you in my selfish world
And the islands, tough and sea-girt, in your mind—
Each a small fight in biographied perspective
That darkly hues the things that you remember.

But that is the way abstractions hinge upon
Dank images of far-off plains and seas;
Nothing can *truly* purely mental be,
Because our brains absorb, from infancy,
Smellings and tastings and sounds and visuals
That leave their souvenirs like empty shells
Clustered along a tide line till we die.

No, I am faced with a problematic you,
Whose tarnished thoughts I want to replace with new.

Unfairnesses

I have to hold my breath when I look out
At the grasses shaking in the autumn wind;
I fear the unfair conclusion that the North
Will arm himself and forthwith sally forth
To spread his snows, death drifts bereft of love,
Wherever you will walk or drive or move.

O, my bewildering antidote to care,
Which manifests its being everywhere,
How can I *not* chain versicles about
The happy neck and incandescent throat
I see when your scarf comes off and shows to me
Those sources of your proud vocality?

And yet there still sounds a subtle augury
That I not overemphasize your quandary.

A Little Swatch of Rain

Maybe there'll be a little swatch of rain
When you come next to visit me again,
And I will want, in vain, to dry your hair,
And I will stand in silence while you pare
Your winter outer clothing from your being,
While I pretend to look elsewhere, unseeing.

Oh, for a moment's liquid lacquered height,
Where you press your body next to mine, despite
Your frenzied vow to never let me hold
Your body in embraces mild or bold!
The terrified oligopoly of "nought"
Is not what any poet sought;

Unless, that is, he has the will to dream
That "nothing" is rarely what it seems to seem.

A Film of You

A continental slowness there would be
In any moving film I made of you.
Who knows what blood would swell your arteries
If you could see yourself the way I do?
Who knows what phantoms of deliberate night
Might run away and die from sheer delight?

And who can say when travails of desire
Might riddle your veins the way they do mine?
And who would criticize the way I feel,
When I feel you watching but then resign
Myself to writing flourishes like these,
Gestures of want beneath a poetese,

Each reaching out to where you stand, stock-still?
You know, I've maybe tried too hard to thrill
To something rampant all your diligence;
I haven't yet dislodged, from all your elegance,
A continental slowness that might stress
How film cannot convey your innerness.

Byronic

Have you no vehicles of innerness
To fight my likening of you to Night
As you walk in winter, Byronic nonetheless,
Through cloisters of calamities of white?

When winter ice bears down its frozen weight
On the bare shoulders of this freezing Earth,
"You walk in Beauty" *might* exaggerate
The confidence with which you sortie forth

'Neath clouds that this winter's cold cannot forsake,
So hang, with their pendant overloads, right down
To touch the embosom'd iciness of the lake,
While you walk on, in your coat of grey and brown,

To where outlandish nightfall calls you home,
And I dare not allow my thoughts to roam.

Exaggerating #1

I cannot see how Earth could be more full
Than it presently is with you upon its orb;
Your gentle self does more than just absorb
What sympathies and generosities pull
You alongside the people that you meet each day.

Earth seems so full that I am dumb with awe;
This Earth, whose machinations go from storms
To fires, would vacuoled be if no reforms
Arose to shut rude Nature's gaping maw;
But you fill this Earth with wondrousness and play;

And yet I'm but half-content to hymn your praise;
I know that exaggerations drive you crazy.
I know that you think I am often lazy,
When I fail poetic licence to erase,
And don't truncate, to truth, hyperbole.

Mightier Than the Pen

When are your hands more mighty than the pen
That hymns them and surveys their soft-like pulp
That capable is of forming joys or, firm,
Appending improper justice to a slap?

Without your hands, my pen is shorn of words;
It writes, with a solemn glumness, of nothing;
But, with your hands, my pen takes secret wings
That no one can see, and takes its stormy flight

Into incredible majesties of skies,
Where only I, in solitary flight,
Bestow my benedictions on your hands
That keep me earthed, while heaven rushes by.

Sonics

I have so little imperturbability
That a twitch becomes a screech and a purr a putrid howl;
Calls that irrevocably tell me to confine
Conjectures within high metaphoric walls, with each
Distinct from the next, fizzle instead to sonic sounds
That clutter the air with reticulated frequencies
And loudnesses doomed to decibel my words like cries;

And it's only expostulating overtones that hang
At chaotic angularities onto tentacles,
Which wriggle from sober words to spear insanities,
That can form foundations firm for every sentiment
And buttress their wordy wilderness with tender feelings,
Tense or relaxed in accordance attuned to your awareness
That those foundations consist of my wishing well for you.

Exaggerating #2

When, as has happened, I happen to invite
Your calumnies by phoning far too late
Over some trifle I can't obliterate,
Because I cannot find a way to overwrite

What had been written but was no longer right,
I feel I am forced, by godforsaken Fate,
A Fury, or Erinys, to exaggerate
And bloat a mere excrescence to a blight.

Endnote

No matter how barbaric be the End—
Sulphurous, cutting off all breath,
Or drenched in meretricious rain—
Over it all will sovereignly reign
My endless unconditioned love for you;

And no matter how a Rapture may fill with bliss,
With worms and daddy-long-legs quiet and still,
And all the world a-choruses a hymn
To the great pontificating Her or Him,
My love for you has music that's more true;

And should neither a whimper nor a bang but silence
Herald the beginning of the End,
A grand grandiloquent parade will hie
Its way across the sky-plain, floating high
And yelling my love for you across its blue.

I'll Write for You

I'll write for you whatever it is
You'd like or need or want;
It can enclothe new mysteries,
In chorus or in chant.

It can move fast or tinker along,
Refurbishment for thought;
It can be rhythmic, impelling, or strong,
Or so weak that it tapers to nought.

It can be high- or low-dwelling, or cute,
Forcing a game from the sky;
It can be earthen and firm and astute,
Or mistily gravitate by;

But whatever it is, it will always ring true,
Because it's a truth that you'll always be you.

Resolution

There's something I dare not put to pen
For fear that that something might happen again,
And I, from my rooftop's height, will fear
That a doom-fraught day will again draw near;

But now I know better, for I have learnt
That the child in me knows, from having been burnt,
That twice is too often, and thus I must shy
From the cloudbanks that pepper my heartbroken sky;

And, avoiding the stigma I'm misunderstood,
No vengeance I'll vent; I'll resolve to do good;
And, in a pretence of being quite unconcerned
That my ego once more has been soiled by being spurned,

I'll trowel a veneer of love unencumbered
Over my days, to ensure they're not numbered.

The Girl of His Dreams

No revelatory mouthings need emerge
From one who feels his mounting feelings surge
At the thought, as much as at her actual sight,
Of the girl he dreams of, daytime, noon, and night;

But what is revealed instead is a steady wealth
Of faded images nurtured back to health
By the thought of the girl he dreams of all the time,
Torrential truths recharged by rabid rhyme.

A Brutal Darkness

And now the brutal darkness sheds its light
And makes what was obscured now clean and bright;
Anomalies you'd thought were sacrosanct
Were simply blindnesses, opaquenesses
Of unclear thought, where only sorrow's waste
Can render life to the unremitting grey
Of knowing you have lost her anyway.

How hard you've worked, poor unbecoming you!
How inexplicable is the morning dew
Of sadness that regales each living blade
Of grass in the gutted quagmire of your mind!
How inexcusable your being so kind
As to spare your other soulmates from the pain
Of seeing you with someone new again!

No sedatives or soporifics lie
In the quiet jungle of her female eye!
I've tried so hard to tempt her unto me,
But all that I've unearthed is jealousy—
In *myself*—so deep it really could achieve
The death-in-life psychologists believe
Is essence of the finest right to grieve.

I've just shut the window against a bitter air
That blows its cold inside this room, to where
I'm sitting with my pen clutched in between
Fingers that whisper of what there might have been
Between us had she brought her fingers near
My hand and taken it as equal peer;
But she had nothing to lose, by losing me, but fear.

When You Phone

How green and softly burning are my thoughts
With life apologetic when you phone!
Whatever it is you say, informative always,
Brings synergy into my surging selfishness.
My replies begin to shake, as if mimetic,
Betraying my secret feelings in their answers.
That is because my physics are not yours;
They do not possess the *savoir faire* and poise
Of your reasoned explanations of your plans
Sociably to engage in conversations
That impel you into a higher role to play
As custodian of your educational maelstrom.
Meanwhile, I am trying to stop the heart-thumps
That linger fitfully on, after you've finished,
Lying in wait for your voice's re-revival.

When You Arrive

Although the sun today is bright and gold,
It's tempered with a wind that's gusty-cold,
And though the towering trees stand fiery-tall,
One's plans to exercise decline and fall;

But the forecast is of brightness, and those trees,
Mustering brilliant colours in that breeze,
Erect a kind of masquerade of glow
That carries us forward to the first-fall snow;

And until that happens, the driving will be good,
Clear-visioned and engine-smooth beneath the hood;
And I will await your smile when you arrive
And cherish how you kick-start my autumn soul alive.

Shh!

Don't aggravate her; never, ever tell
How her body sends you to a kind of Hell,
Where torments lace their emotions up your legs,
And you know well your writing's hit its dregs.

So pleasure her; tell how it always seems
That a welter-burst of high sporadic dreams
Plays on the sides and billows of your mind,
With happiness unfettered, freed, and kind;

And then cool down; be dignified, mature;
Portray her as ideal and as demure;
Write how she bares the universe's head
And crowns it with fantasticness instead;

And then stop cold, until a later hour
Sends you a floral hymn to fill her bower.

If You Went

I fear a fatal infinite conjunction
Of dangers crowding on my certitude
That, if you went, there's nowhere I could go
To compensate your loss; I would just stay
And watch the tremulous sunsets fade to night
And see the early stars peer, Earth-like, down
Through moving banks of cloud; and I'd look up
At where the moon hung lamp-like in the sky
As if in a tent of manifested dark;
And, in mind, I would turn away from those
Augurs and signs of a fretful universe
And slowly start to stroll, with blood
Filling my breathing breast with glancing grief
And filling my brooding brain with emptiness.

What Are You?

Are you bewitched, or merely commonplace?
If, on an afternoon, the sun shines low
Upon your hair, so that it shines not, nor
Do its amber tresses hint of sunlight's glow,

The answer is, "You're normal, commonplace,"
But if, on an evening, the sun rains down
Gleamings to glamorize your lovely hair,
As if a god arranged to place his crown

To decorate the ambitious ambience
Of yourself, then I would fall, subservient,
Before the upstanding womanhood, in light
Parnassian, that you would represent;

Yours are the glories of a gilded state
Where "you are bewitched" means "you are truly great."

Looking Ahead?

I look to when I'll not be shy
To look you in your limpid eye
And feel no backwardness in me
Where once it was, explicitly.

With the one I'm with, I do not aggress
Because the occasioned storm and stress
Can filter like poison through her life,
And I'll wind up without a wife.

I look to when I'll understand
When and when not to take your hand
And yearn for that simple, soulful day
When all the pain has passed away.

Wantings

Accretive in the passive mood
Are wantings to be understood,
Not in a psychological way,
But in a common humanhood.

What things I want, because they bring
Me pleasures strong enough to sing,
Are what I also want to share
With you, at all times, everywhere;

And yet I cannot hymn them here;
Too new they'd be to you. I'd fear
Your resistance to art's divinities,
Its insistence on sublimities;

But maybe my fear need not for long persist;
Sublime is the very fact that you exist.

Wishful Thinking

I see you in an epic light,
Like the light that currently cascades
From a breeze-blue sky to the hilltop's height
And highlights the treetops' palisades

Of masses of tuft-like reds and greens
And yellows, each picked, in spotlight glare,
Out from the scything near-ravines
That rift the dimpled hillside's stair.

Thus contrasted, the autumn's coloured leaves
Seem like toys festooning a childhood floor,
Blazing out once before the snow bereaves
And silences the fall for one year more;

And you seem to blaze, before the snows appear,
As if enchantress-you might let me near.

The Landscape That I View

I live the very landscape that I view;
I look at it and, always, think of you.
When wild, ebullient towerings of cloud
Cover the sky, I idolize the proud
Upliftings of my soaring mind when I
Compare you to that high, ecstatic sky.
But when the light grows dim, as night comes down—
Etching its razor'd blackness on the town,
Sharpening the buildings and their ledges
Until their contrast-vivid coloured edges
Dazzle the world, with regal golds and blacks,
Arithmetics designèd to relax,
Manipulated on a map called *me*—
I huddle down beneath night's blanketry
And know that—*phwoosh*!—all of that will fizz away,
If you prefer *absentia* to play.

Evolving

I love you with a terrible disorder
That lubricates, yet stultifies, my mind,
As if the feeling that I feel for you
Were also felt by all of humankind;

And though an intemperate sky may overflood
This Earth that is a monument to space,
I know that my disorder's an affliction
Whose purpose is to propagate the race.

If Only ...

And spring brings next a copper beech in red,
With flowering-cherry pink and white ahead,
While the leaf-greens of a myriad matching hues
Bluster and curl their presences on my views
Of the hillside's re-arrangement and re-tread.

And will you be there, accoutred bright and new,
When I open the door and confront the glorious you,
Slender and poised like a new-green flowering
Of a hillside sapling, glowing in new spring,
Standing firm, and bursting to grow, and to be true

To your self-containing harness and restraint
From expressing any semblance of complaint.

Against the Grain

When nobody wanted it to rain,
And yet it did,
It went against an inner grain,
An aptitude,

To blame "God's will," as if to say
That, had you prayed,
"Rain, O rain, please go away"
It would've stayed;

When nobody wanted you to go,
And yet you went,
I searched for, high and far and low,
Impediment

To stop your vanishing away
From where I stood;
But could not think of a single way
Both Right and Good.

Exaggerating #3

If I this further thought to you might now express,
Although the favoured shades of night are overstarred
By barriers of blockage on your part, I shall,
Unheeding, still express its open-ended essence
In somewhat addled nouns, the better to conceal
The upended regrets, the dishevelled hopes, the meagre shards
Of the superfluities for which I've fought so long
And hardily, in a stream that has fallen to turmoil.

And yet, and yet … dotted purveyances of yet,
And yet … aggrieved and unconcluded, dated before
Anything like a birth where I could see you whole
And unpartitioned, undivided by clothing's seasons …
These inadvertent spoils of overdone linguistics
Stand like spectral columns supporting your temple's roof.

Four Triptychs

One:
Such grief now spreads, I'm sickened deep inside,
And no man knows how this can feel or be,
Unless he knows why her affection's died.

Two:
I crave the sullen colour of her dress,
But it has gone, and all that I can do
Is crave that sullen colour slightly less.

Three:
Within the darkness of the night's caress,
I rise and write an abstract, then return
And see a pillow moist with nothingness.

Four:
How can I go out to greet the sun
In its full blaze, from star to shining star,
When it reminds me of a smoking gun?

Inhibited

Silence is the only response to the question
Of why I did not smile at the suggestion,
Conveyed in bodied move, without a word,
That you on me approval had conferred.

This Past Week

A clarity upthrust the afternoon
To an island of non-drizzle this past week;
So dark had its environment of days
Become, in the week of absence from strong sunshine,
That that moment's clarity had cast a cloak
Of seeming sunniness on its surrounds
And made that paltry stand-out afternoon
Into a guest of some hilarity
In the tawdry crowd of daytimes all around it;
And so it was that I saw your coming visit
That afternoon as light within my busy-ness
(And, even more so, yours); and when you phoned
To say you could not spread deliciousness
Over that afternoon, I downed the phone,
Obstreperously cursing all of Nature.

A Day Too Long

A day too long
Before she phones,
And I think she's gone.

An hour too late,
With snow in the air,
And I speculate

She's taken her leave;
Delay always leads
My mind to believe

She's no longer there;
She'll have taken wing
On the empty air,

And gone and left,
Leaving me
Sad and bereft,

Grieving, adrift,
Deludedly daft,
And mortally miffed.

Overcast

So heavy with the dark of over-headed pressure,
The clouds, Calliope-like, upsurge, while under,
Rayed from the wide horizon's brightening landscape,
Sunlight and radiance tear the clouds asunder.

Your life and mine are overclouded heavily;
Knowledge fattens its brains upon our thought;
Insanity rakes its mordent bits from the pathways
That strew their byways wherever they are brought.

I want to clean you from the academic clutter
That bristles like raw fingers on a gun,
Aimed to destroy a truth that's inconvenient,
Aimed to make sure that destruction means it's won;

And in your sweet eyes I see the shine of ages
Harden when tyranny looms, outrageous.

I Know You'll Phone

I know you're going to phone tonight
And know that when you do,
No matter what you think or say,
I'll extra-sense how you

Look on the end of the phone out there—
Maybe in bedtime gear,
Or outdoor clothes you entered with,
Or stuff you just like to wear;

And my mind is a-split into two parts:
The rational nice guy who speaks,
And the fuming, fomenting crusader
Who's awaited your ear-words for weeks.

New Desires

Pools of light are formed, like slippered decks,
On the long, grey floor of the grey-flecked upper lake,
When sunshine resurrects its tattered self
And peeks between the rifts of the parting clouds;
And I am trying to find what earthly moral
Would be apt and fitted to decorate this scene,
With something profound or pathetic or unprosaic,
But I cannot; the only lesson from these swathes
Of sunlight billowing down from the one-time storm
Onto these sheeted yellow planks of light
Is that losing one's love is often camouflaged
By islands of new desires in a sea of loss.

High Winds

High winds streak down upon my lonely self,
A wandering person, I, beside my balustrade;
Chief shine the white streaks of the windy sky,
Glad at the orchestrations they have made
Of cumulonimbic herringbones up high.

Somehow, it did seem somewhat of a strain
To new-neologize these wispy wreaths of white,
As if a lighter glow suffused the blue
With which I contemplated how too slight
Would be the chance I'd ever reach your *you*;

But it didn't seem a strain when, after a while,
I likened the way I like to see you smile
To the way a cloud that tried to dominate the Earth
Was broken apart by a sunlight's unconstrainèd mirth.

Other Musings

Cross-Currents

I opened up her beauty's bitter gauze
And saw no wondering;
The veiling lilts of her soft opal eyes
Had nothingness beneath them;
A screeching beauty in a heartfelt hall,
She stood, as did the other guests, conversing.

Like a fleet but blocked transaction, I
Stood, as twofold as a Janus;
Her beauty beseeched the firmaments to smile,
While with one side of me, joy
Furnished the ornamentations to their play,
And I felt old fears glow cold and melt away;

But her utter enwrapment in a sanity
Born of achievement, a firmness,
Knowing she knew the right one, spread
A dreadful welter of contempt across
Her puzzled mind when she saw just how estranged
I, desolate, felt in her social assuredness.

Uninhibited?

It's strange how free I feel to take your hand,
Although I know it isn't really kind
To do so while I'm still a step behind
You and your man, whom I well understand.

Verses like these make mockery of threes;
Two's company, three's a crowd, they say,
And yet my instinct pulls me right away
To stand near you as often as I please;

And my architectural siftings through these sands
Of idiosyncratic push-and-pulls
Of wants and moods and monosyllables
Do me no good; they are just buts and ands

That dot (or speck?) these angry flocks of lines
That crow my unrespectable designs.

A Rumour

A cause for casual murmur were we once,
But nobody knew the cause was secret you;
You came to my office once so very late
That silence was like a ball of empty sound
That rolled the hallway's lengthway all night through.

The door was closed, and I held you almost close,
But bewildered was I by treachery of faith,
Knowing my idle heart was fraught with fear
That, if I were to win you, I might lose
Another whose spectre hovered like a wraith

Over that lengthy hallway and my books;
But a sudden sound perturbed the atmosphere;
A janitor came by; I knew that he could hear
Movements behind my door and, of course, next day,
In my presence, he took the greatest pains to say,
Somebody'd been there very late at night,
Gossip that gave him infinite delight.

Once More, Again

So many rhymes have filtered from my pen
That a yawn I stifle when, once more, again,
I lift this blackened ballpoint to refocus
On what could be logistic hocus-pocus
Designed to make thinking women laugh with scorn
At something over-close to thought-game porn;

But now my pen is lifted, caringly,
To treat with respect I lavish sparingly,
And make clear to you that I'm hanging back,
Not wishing to say there's something I lack
That you can give me but, instead, to write
That I want to give you more of what's your right:

To be accompanied, again, once more,
Be an entrepreneur who's also a troubadour.

Seeing Someone

I know a woman younger than myself
Who, nevertheless, looks older than do I;
And I saw a woman estimably younger
Than she was, and who caught my eager eye.

Tactful towards the elder of the two,
I made no move the younger to apprehend;
And off she vanished, leaving the two of us
To wonder what it takes to make a friend

Delectable as someone fully holdable,
When age wears such impermeable gear
That only the eyes betray persistent sensings
Of ambient attractions spoiled by fear.

Oh, where did she go, that eager younger woman
Who, if she knew *my* age, might wax inhuman?

Many Years Later

I see you, many years later, and see that still
Your eyes can lambaste me with their lucent beauty,
Till I flinch, and want to drink from them until
Longing is quenched by sufficiency or duty.

I know this truth to be self-evident,
Because once, in a crowd, my eye was caught, unaware,
By a tiny movement of a well-cut skirt of a kind
That causes a watcher to suddenly stop and stare,

Just for a moment, long enough for her
To move more clearly into his line of fire,
And lower her eyes to let him see and adore her,
While both are scheming to vivify desire

By continuing meeting—but you were by my side;
To have left with her would have been conscience suicide.

Poignant

Another poignant catch on a crowded subway—
An adolescent, sitting there in peace,
Felt moved to move her eyes towards my *me*-ness,
And I, responding, dared to move my lips,
Outreaching with a tiny smile towards her cheeks,
And she replied with the tiniest possible smile
Compatible with our future non-acquaintance.

Nightlife

Now, as the nighttime leases out long hours,
Awake, I do not let its sultry calm
Bewilder me with feckless fantasies
That only serve high gold for fractioned minutes
Before they lapse away; I look at the night
Whose blackness broods behind a pane of glass;
And, indoors, the lights, spiral or semi-globular,
Lighten the painted walls with luminance,
And I see their glow atop this testament
To my appalled ferocity of tenure
Of a grip-hold on the possibility,
Persuaded by my mad mentality,
That you might hold me in a stronger grip
Because I'd then confound all admonition.

A Philadelphia Story

Centred upon vicissitudes of ire,
That lie, in turn, upon vicissitudes
Of fear that all my fantasies expire
In new and bitter waves of angry moods,

My mind leaps out to when I once frequented
Girls on a bus or train or in the street;
So many differences, yet each presented
An invitation I dare scarce repeat.

In Philadelphia, I did once have the chance,
And stood up to walk with her, but found
That paralysis seemed to strike like happenstance,
And I could not lift my feet from off the ground;

Because you were there in mind, wagging a finger;
She watched me stop, she smiled, but did not linger.

Drabness

For me, all women dressed in dullish green,
Or tawdry, shabby brown, electric are;
I'm tempted to strut, to serenade their star,
And indeed they might listen, knowing they'd been seen;

But not a hint of a wilful come-on-hither
Is shown by a nesting bird who hides her young;
A nurturing Nature has providentially hung
Deliberate drabness on every female feather;

So, when I detect such dullness of attire,
I know a woman stands there I'll desire;
I might sit in a corner, huddled o'er my lyre,
And try to tune it up ten pitches higher;

But dare I move? Dare I hone in on her?
I ought, but do not—to caution I defer.

Contact

I want your love to fall on top of me,
Or take my back as a rest-place for your arm,
Or feel an intangible, but pleading, tug
On the outward sleeve of my overbearing parka
And know that your unconscious moves at last.

Days, months, years have passed us, fruitless, by;
I do not know what tiny jungle formed
In your all-hail-the-victor! seeing of your world;
But that one moment's counterpoise that held,
In its softness, that outreach of your unwary arm

That gripped, but dared not hold, my outer coat,
Has left a memory that might outlast your life.

The Interpretation of Dreams

I dare not sap what's rancid from my dreams;
Dreams are too often polyglots of fate
That erect something beautiful and gloss-sublime
That symbolizes what you do *not* want;
A warning it can be: you've thrown away,
For reasons so moral as to raise contempt,
The affections of someone who respected you,
And left her, leery and lurching, in a limbo.

It was after that that I dreamed of her as bride
In a gorgeous ethnic wedding, standing there
Full-face and smiling in my face, ecstatic;
But when, years later, I re-met that bride,
'Twas not to me she was espoused, it was
Another, and her mien was beatific;
And earlier faults she'd had when we had parted
Had disappeared, perfecting her revenge
On me for my misshapen enterprise.

A Memory

A long and weary many miles ago,
Were space to be restructured into years,
I ventured with you to a havoc-land,
Wherein were ventures intermixed with tears
—All in a lonely lostness of rebound.

One night, I remember, I drove to where you lived,
And knocked on your door; you did not let me in.
Someone more stable than me sat on your chair,
(Or so, at least, I guessed); in thick chagrin
I bumbled back, through the slowly falling snow,

To my car and drove home, in quiet despond,
Crestfallen, tired of my dull and ashen mind,
Hands on the steering wheel at ten past ten,
Eyes on a glowing nightfall, semi-blind.

Growth

A wafted wind can make a wayward cloud
Stretch in a lengthwise drift across the sky
When the evening sun is reddening for its rest;
Along the hilltop's crest the cloud is blown,
As if a fire had started and its smoke
Were spread by rivulets of sunset's breath
Across the horizontals I could see;

And so, like a fire whose real-life rising smoke,
Undaunted, grows to a trailing robe that moves,
Gathering force until it finally billows,
Inflaming fears of a one-time conflagration
Whose onwardness is quite unquenchable,
I feel that what is, just now, a tiny hope
Of wanting to be with you, might grow incendiary.

Because ...

So-and-so, agèd sixty-three,
Is just the kind of girl for me,
But what a rotter I would be,
Because she's married.

She is tall and fine and spruce,
With vivid talk when she lets loose,
But for her, of course, I have no use,
Because she's married.

Oh, how I envy that lucky man
Who talks to her whene'er he can,
While, musing, I bring up the van,
Because she's married.

Just two lines more my soul inclines
To add to this poem's fourteen lines:
All gone to pot are my designs,
Because she's married.

Knowledge

A band of nearly sacrilegious fire
Spreads knife-like underneath a ridge of black,
A tonguing of the sun into the thunder,
The knowledge that I'll never get her back.

Space and Sky

I Remember This Place ...

A herringbone wind sprawls high,
Scoring the sky
With clouds that look like cloaks of spreading fur.

Sunset is happening, but no red
Seems to spread
Colours that look like blood on the sabled fur.

A sunset white is a symbol of growing black
Over the back
Of the broadening ridge of herringbonèd fur.

A wind-blow high in the overdomed sky
Will probably die,
As the arch-backed night flies by the cloud.

And the cloud will shake itself and curl,
Like a girl,
Into a sun-shell world.

Yellow Flowers

For some unconscious reason, all the gods
Have taken wagers and accepted odds
That the flowers be yellow on my patio,
Where, wildly, they spontaneously grow.

Thus speaks Induction from her musty books;
If yellow sprouts in August from the nooks
That pierce the concrete slabs on which I tread,
September will bring me yellow, never red

Or blue, or green, or tangerine, or teal.
So imagine me wondering what the gods might feel
When, in October, a sudden burst of leaves
Broke into purples, amethysts, and mauves,

So achingly surprising, where I stepped,
That I thought the hollow yellows must have wept.

Although the Day Began

Although the day began
With a devastating spread of hues and shades,
With cloud-made pillars darkened as reflections,
And with glints of icy steel against the golds
Of a dawn-break's reddening,

A craze of lake-top light drops
Now hinted that the moving waves were catching
Gleanings of the silver light behind,
Cloud rolls that moved slowly through the morning,
And then faded, as the hours advanced

To lunchtime, to a sky
Wisped with white faintness across its blue horizons,
While the waters glittered and flashed; but I sat down,
Puzzled as to why, three lines ago,
"Lunchtime" had beaten "noon."

Downing the Sun

The sun and the moon were in the sky
Together;
The sun was a flattened orbal disc,
Dazzling;
The moon was a nearly spherical shell,
Convexicoid;
And the sky that framed them both was blue
All through.

To be surprised to see a setting sun
Together with
A hesitant moon, enchanted from the sky
By tricks
Of light reverberant from febrile Earth,
Is to drown
The rudimentary alchemies of space
In grace.

Morningrise

So steep a grid of sunlight fell upon
The hillside as the rising sun came up,
That, crystalline, the sun's illumination
Festooned dark walls with windows and with stone,
While, at the farthest edge of the lakeside eastward,
A building rose I'd never seen before.

Four hours later, the sky was unhazed blue,
Cloudlets wandered their ways like lazy fleeces,
Sailboats dotted the lake, and far away,
Exquisite tiny dots of white lay near
The opposite shore of the lake, where, long and low,
A colourless stretch of rolling surface lay
That rolled like hills to those who rowed thereon.

Alone, a Boat

Alone, a boat, near ripple-less, propels
Itself along a straight-line course, out far
Beneath an overcasting sky of grey,
Alone, sole mover on that quiet lake,
Whose coloured greys deploy the risks of rain;
And yet, when the sun shines on it near the land,
That grey turns into brown, like a mass of sand.

Perhaps it's a police-boat, showing its upper hand
With its purposeful progression, showing its command
Of the watercraft the lakeshore can sustain,
As it smoothly holds its path, with meagre wake,
Towards some destination not too far away;
An aqueous equivalent of a cruising car
Designed to intimidate all ne'er-do-wells

Who score the scrappy sea with hints of crimes
Designed to take advantage of hard times.

Horizons Stretch

Horizons stretch and watch the dappled sky,
Stumble while they stretch and try to cry;
But mute are their earthly mouthfuls; not a sound
Comes out from their dried and overburdened ground.
So only a silence crowns the horizon's rim,
And not a sound to sunset's ear can climb.
Riveted is Earth to a dramaturge named Life.

And Night, when moontide sweeps the darkened table
Of treetops, lined with its silver and its sable,
Who lay their ferny tips in pleasant rest
Against the moonlight's round and pleasing breast,
Spreads out a silence like to that of Day,
When horizons want to cry and run away.
Riveted is Life to iconoclastic Earth.

Question

How could I *not* assimilate a sky
That seemed to move itself (so fast surged up
Its massing clouds onto the land
From the wide, flat lake and mistiness they'd left)
To the moving tumult of each week I'd waited,
Where all events surged upward out of Time,
Then fell to mere ephemeralities,
While the target and pure solidity of my dream
Stayed soft and firm, like the clouds that evanesced
From the lake's hard depths and coldly boiling fumes?

The Rustle of Spring

If white clouds mean spring's meaning is not marred,
And darker clouds mean rain is on its way,
What do *these* mean, midwintery clouds of grey
That wander over a blue sky, undeterred?

They have a pink, as if noontime, underneath
Their mottled spreads of white and dark and gloom;
It seems as if a summertide might loom,
And hope accost a winter's steady breath.

It is as if this cold were breached and riven;
It is as if, living with life once more,
A spring or a summer were to gear for war,
And shout to heroes, tired from being brave,

That warming would arrive: a sky-long call
That resentment could be beaten after all.

Artwar

The night when Nightfall's beauty lent
Inchoate breath to a breaking Eastern sky
Was also the night when bright Aurora sent
Angelic waves of wings to overfly
The Earth, whose towns, alacrified, stood by,
Waiting to see if they needed to fight, and why.

Beauty unreal can cloud an evil's face;
The night winds of the wondrous Universe,
Pretending to spread holiness through Space,
Instead reminded Time of times still worse,
When humankind had felt its hopes reverse
And Beauty that was real had gasped a curse

As down she went in helpless scrimmages
With unreal Beauty's swarms of images.

Rocked in the Cradle of the Sky

Each landscape brings a new non-failing day;
Higher the hill stands when the sky is dark,
Or mist spreads its archways over the sleeping park,
And the hill's horizon stands stark against the grey;

But the light, when it comes, can cause, with a single ray,
The somnolent trees to bluster and flap their leaves,
As if to hint how that gleam of light reweaves
A summer's idols into an autumn day;

And, cradled upon the static stateliness
Of the hill as it stands impassively and still,
Waiting for clouds to drift from the lake to fill
Its grey with puffs of whitened seamlessness—

Cradled up there in a sky that waits and waits,
Maybe there'll float a bronzed receptacle,
Utterly fictional, clad in the kind of spectacle
Only a child in an opera creates—

Cradled up there, I am trying to say, is nothing;
The sky goes on, reacting to the sun's
White benedictions spreading in orisons
Determined by the cloud-claps' redirectioning—

The sky goes on as constant as a sea
That sweeps mankind and womankind along
In a current, not quite as powerful as song,
But powerful enough to conquer me.

Thus Spake the God of Snow

The whole of my hill is a sprinkled ferny feather
Sealed in snow, the feather of a white bird,
Intoxicated in its preen of white.

A battle with a problem is the finding
Of a starting point, the like of which, once found,
Yields wonder at one's wondrous depth of slowness.

Ungrateful mortals, stir your vitals now!
Nothing can stir your mind to whitened heights
The like of which I can invoke, when I cover,

With glazing, freezing hilts of belted snow,
The arms of the branchlike crystalinity
Of my hill with a beauty that blinds all ye below!

Memorials

A Remembrance of Esther

Searching, as I daily do, for riches
To decorate my mornings' sleepy movings
From coffee to food and paper to TV,
I recall, within a jubilation's joy,
Mornings that bathed the mid part of my life.
Hidden among those mornings were her yawns,
Her somewhat tousled hair, her pattered steps
Between the bed and bathroom, and the doors
Concealing hanging clothes and laid-out shoes;
I remember how she adored to see the sunlight.

Esther's Grave

There she lies, thick and filtered through
With heavy earth made heavier by the dew,
While by the hillside where she rests and sleeps,
A train its tryst with Punctuality keeps.

I am on that train; I see high trees
Rising above the place she lies at ease;
She'll never know that I am on that train
Sliding towards her, then pulling away again;

But I cannot retreat from what she means
To me, when I remember early scenes
When she walked with me, on that heavy earth and planned
A mutual graveyard bedside on that land.

Her Name

An unimportant man may die unknown
And his name be lost in Earth's oblivion,
Did not the pointing pierce script on his stone
Denote his place in our dominion.

Humanity's realm can likewise hold no store
By a woman's name, forgotten like cold air
That blows, then fades, upon a rocky shore,
Visited by no one not from there;

But on a headstone, glittering with frost,
Her name would be flaunted when the gleaming ice,
Perfusing into springtime, would be lost;
A name so valued none could name its price.

Others have raised, in odes and monuments,
The names of femininities ethereal
Up to a sky where Venus documents
Their loves and sacrifices magisterial;

But Venus is paltry purveyor of her worth;
No straggling document, celestial, stands
So regal as to hymn her time on Earth
With all the adornments that her stay demands.

For she broke faith with a fiction here on Earth
That Inequality reigns where love should be:
"What Woman wants is accessory to birth;
What Man wants is excess of venery."

She broke this faith by being my paramour,
Ready to clamber our married living-tree
Up to its endmost heights, where loss of power
Adjunctive is to loss of potency;

Yet still insisted, with unfeigned honesty,
That what I wanted also be part of her.
This is my homage to her modesty;
This is my paean to her character.

There is no doubt that knighthood's errant past,
With its dominance of courtly word and speech
Between the genders, failed to overcast
That urgency that always tries to breach

Resistances, rendering them banal,
Despite the rules they offer shaken men
Whose dream is of an endless bacchanal
Wherein they live, unleashed, in a lechers' den.

Yet knighthood's speech remains aloft, alive;
It's there in the pen that every poet wields.
Each puddled splotch of ink is meant to thrive
Whenever a woman to a poem yields,

And likewise, though its novelty be rife
With mental hesitations unexpected,
Whenever her husband has poems from his wife,
His body will to hers be genuflected.

No end is there to lively rhyming reason;
It flows as from a cataract from Heaven,
Sprawling into streams for every season,
Like a river that runs and grades its banks to even.

Nor is there any end to fantasies;
One person plays a part in countless plays,
From rhetoric formed from whispered niceties
To acrobatic moves and proud displays.

Nor can a ban be placed on imaging;
Coloured arrays betray imagination
That paints with frescos hours of lingering,
Until it finds pellucid peroration

Of solidly mixed transfusions of incitement
To stop and stay, or onward press to the end.
Both are inaugurations of excitement;
Both into bold denouements vividly blend.

The March of 2012 seemed shorn of wind
Except where the lakeshore stopped the moving waves;
The cemetery's sun inland was twinned
With spring to bind new summers to the graves.

The day was bright; a cavalcade of green
Filled out the spaces spread between the tombs;
A lawn stretched from the road to where she'd been
Blessed and interred; inspired, incipient blooms

Welcomed me wordlessly as I walked to where
I could see her name new-graven on blue stone;
The letters were carved in black and seemed to glare
With impertinent brightness in that midday sun;

And everything she'd meant to me sang bold,
Aloud from her name as it glittered in the noon,
Expressing her self in skeins of melodic gold
Varnished with shades whose shadows would vanish soon.

I was begirt so tightly by my thought
Of how we had walked here long ago to plan
Our resting ground, that I felt tagged and caught
In a net like a prey known only to a man

Who'd already known a resting place in life.
There, he'd been free from any fear he'd lose
The sleeping form, beside him, of his wife;
But should she die, he'd once more have to choose

Whomever's substitution seemed to him
A rated equal to what his life had been;
But choice seemed impoverished, because the whim
Of each potential partner who seemed keen

Would leave him feeling never quite in charge;
Women of his age had come to know
How marriages mould ways to camouflage
Vexations that can, independent, grow

From quotidian encounters with their spouses;
How could he countermand such irritants,
Except by patience, whose calmness would endow
His answers with a tactful elegance?

Or would his reticence be judged as lack
Of humour or of general social grace?
Would his new spouse allow him to go back
To mental depths of thought, or would she trace

To thinking his reluctance to behave
In that open and easy, unresentful way—
That he would need, should the need arise, to save
Their marriage from that fabled rainy day?

All these are wedlock issues that can curse
A marriage from the day both spouses swear
Conjointly that, for better or for worse,
They'll stay together, with unremitting care,

Faithful not only in deeds but also mind,
Preserving all the hopes they'd had of good.
Or would reversals lead to undesigned
Lacuna-riddled spoils of singlehood?

I solemnly entreat your memory,
Wherever in the aether it may be,
To cast your spyglass on my life-to-be,
To track the trite meanderings of me;

Take me away from cliché or from brand
Of metaphoric clinging unto thee;
Track me as I sift, in shifting sand,
Time-loggings of the times we used to see

Each other as protection from the crowd;
And track my renewing hopes there might be three:
Me in the real, you in immortal shroud,
And somebody new I'll thank unceasingly.

CPSIA information can be obtained at www.ICGtesting.com
Printed in the USA
LVOW13s0341051113

359968LV00001B/34/P